WHOLE WIDE WORLD
LEANING TOWER OF PISA

by Kristine Spanier, MLIS

pogo

Ideas for Parents and Teachers

Pogo Books let children practice reading informational text while introducing them to nonfiction features such as headings, labels, sidebars, maps, and diagrams, as well as a table of contents, glossary, and index.

Carefully leveled text with a strong photo match offers early fluent readers the support they need to succeed.

Before Reading

- "Walk" through the book and point out the various nonfiction features. Ask the student what purpose each feature serves.
- Look at the glossary together. Read and discuss the words.

Read the Book

- Have the child read the book independently.
- Invite him or her to list questions that arise from reading.

After Reading

- Discuss the child's questions. Talk about how he or she might find answers to those questions.
- Prompt the child to think more. Ask: Did you know about the Leaning Tower of Pisa before reading this book? What more would you like to learn about it?

Pogo Books are published by Jump!
5357 Penn Avenue South
Minneapolis, MN 55419
www.jumplibrary.com

Copyright © 2022 Jump!
International copyright reserved in all countries.
No part of this book may be reproduced in any form without written permission from the publisher.

Library of Congress Cataloging-in-Publication Data

Names: Spanier, Kristine, author.
Title: Leaning Tower of Pisa / by Kristine Spanier, MLIS.
Description: Minneapolis, MN: Jump!, Inc., [2022]
Series: Whole wide world
Includes index. | Audience: Ages 7-10
Identifiers: LCCN 2021028645 (print)
LCCN 2021028646 (ebook)
ISBN 9781636903132 (hardcover)
ISBN 9781636903149 (paperback)
ISBN 9781636903156 (ebook)
Subjects: LCSH: Leaning Tower (Pisa, Italy)—
Juvenile literature.
Pisa (Italy)—Buildings, structures, etc.—Juvenile literature.
Classification: LCC NA5621.P716 S63 2022 (print)
LCC NA5621.P716 (ebook) | DDC 725/.970945551—dc23
LC record available at https://lccn.loc.gov/2021028645
LC ebook record available at https://lccn.loc.gov/2021028646

Editor: Jenna Gleisner
Designer: Molly Ballanger

Photo Credits: Jim_Pintar/iStock, cover; Fernando Ferrari/Shutterstock, 1; k86/Shutterstock, 3; Alberto Masnovo/Shutterstock, 4; Balate Dorin/Shutterstock, 5; RefinedPictures/iStock, 6-7; Bogdan Lazar/iStock, 8; herraez/iStock, 9; gehringj/iStock, 10-11; Aum Studio/Shutterstock, 12-13; Shutterstock, 14; Giulio Andreini/Getty, 15; SamuelBrownBG/iStock, 16-17; John_Silver/Shutterstock, 18-19; Alphabetman/Shutterstock, 19; Cumberland/Shutterstock, 20-21; Robert Hoetink/Shutterstock, 23.

Printed in the United States of America at Corporate Graphics in North Mankato, Minnesota.

TABLE OF CONTENTS

CHAPTER 1

A COMPLEX IN PISA

In the year 1064, the people of Pisa, Italy, began building a **cathedral**. It is made of marble. It has **arches** and **columns**.

cathedral

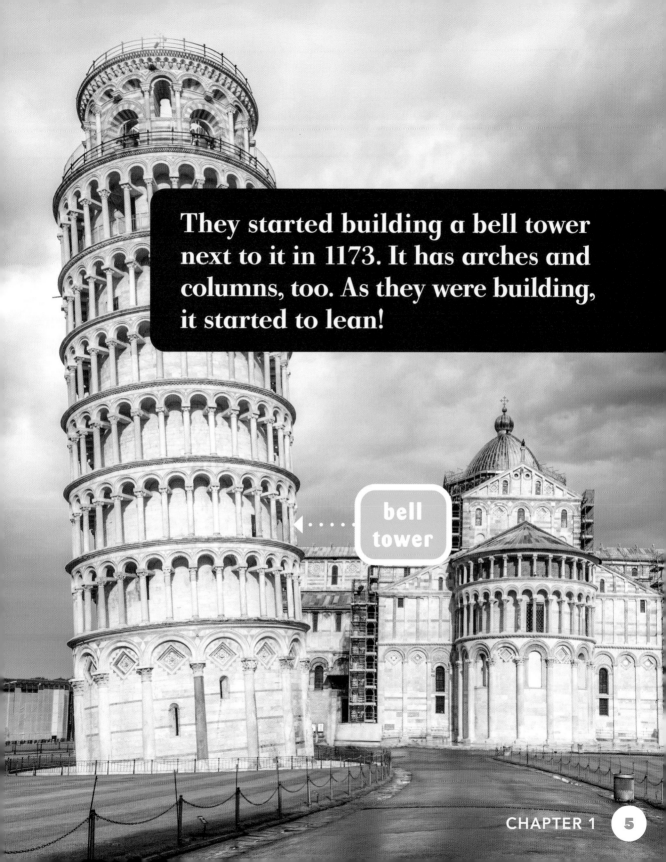

They started building a bell tower next to it in 1173. It has arches and columns, too. As they were building, it started to lean!

bell tower

cemetery

baptistry

The cathedral and bell tower are part of a **complex**. A **baptistry** and cemetery are nearby. All of the buildings here lean. But the tower leans the most. What went wrong?

CHAPTER 2

BUILDING THE BELL TOWER

The Arno River runs through Pisa. Water from the river makes the ground here soft.

Arno River

The tower's **foundation** was set just 10 feet (3.0 meters) into the ground. This wasn't deep enough for the weight of the tower. It wasn't strong enough to hold the tower upright. It began to sink and lean.

Builders tried to fix the lean. How? New stories were made taller on the short side. But the extra weight made it sink even more!

Builders stopped. **Engineers** worked to solve the problem. They drilled holes in the base. They filled them with cement. It didn't work.

DID YOU KNOW?

There were many wars in Italy during this time. Building stopped for more than 100 years. This helped fix the lean. How? It let the ground under the tower flatten. It might have saved the tower from falling over!

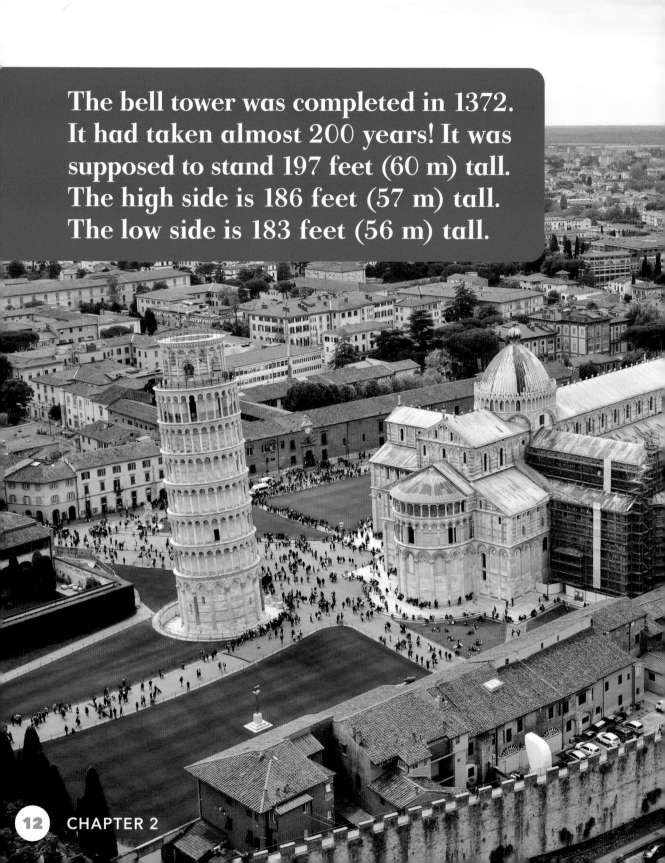

The bell tower was completed in 1372. It had taken almost 200 years! It was supposed to stand 197 feet (60 m) tall. The high side is 186 feet (57 m) tall. The low side is 183 feet (56 m) tall.

TAKE A LOOK!

The bell tower has eight stories. It has 207 columns. Take a look at the other parts!

BELL CHAMBER

ARCH

COLUMN

STORY

GROUND FLOOR

CHAPTER 3

THE LEANING TOWER TODAY

The Civic Tower in Pavia, Italy, **collapsed** in 1989. People feared this would happen to Pisa's tower. It was closed to visitors in 1990.

Workers removed soil from under the high side. They drained water from the soil, too. The ground started to settle. The lean decreased by 17 inches (43 centimeters).

The project was completed in 2001. Visitors could finally return. The tower continued to straighten on its own until 2008. The lean decreased by another two inches (5.1 cm).

Engineers say the tower will remain **stable** for at least 200 years.

WHAT DO YOU THINK?

People have spent a lot of time trying to fix the tower. Do you think they should have just started over? Why or why not?

bell chamber

A marble staircase leads to the **bell chamber**. It is almost 300 steps! At the top, people can look out over Pisa.

Seven bells are in the chamber. The largest weighs almost 8,000 pounds (3,630 kilograms)!

Many people take fun
photos with the tower.
Would you like to visit?

WHAT DO YOU THINK?

The city of Pisa is known for the Leaning Tower. What is your town or city known for? Have you visited it?

QUICK FACTS & TOOLS

Pavia •

FRANCE

Arno River

Pisa

Rome

ITALY

Adriatic Sea

Tyrrhenian Sea

N
W ✛ E
S

LEANING TOWER OF PISA

Location: Pisa, Italy

Height:
186 feet (57 m) on high side
183 feet (56 m) on low side

Years Built: 1173 to 1372

Past Use: bell tower

Current Use: bell tower and visitor attraction

Number of Visitors Each Year: around 5 million

GLOSSARY

arches: Curved shapes over openings.

baptistry: A building used for baptisms.

bell chamber: A room containing one or more bells hung from their frames.

cathedral: A large and important church.

collapsed: Fell down suddenly.

columns: Pillars that help support a building.

complex: A group of buildings that are near each other and are used for similar purposes.

engineers: People who are specially trained to design and build machines or large structures.

foundation: The part of a structure that connects to the ground and supports and anchors the structure.

stable: Firmly fixed in place.

INDEX

TO LEARN MORE

Finding more information is as easy as 1, 2, 3.

1. Go to www.factsurfer.com
2. Enter "LeaningTowerofPisa" into the search box.
3. Choose your book to see a list of websites.

FACT SURFER